The cover illustation by is entitled
“The Unseen.”

It comments on who we do and do not see, and why. Some of those most commonly unseen (whom some may also prefer not to see), are depicted as faceless. If the viewer does see them, do they see them as a symbol of what they believe them to represent or are they seen in order to be proactively discounted or rejected entirely?

The seen and unseen together comprise society, as does how or whether the viewer views.

Do we see similar situations equally or does it depend on the “who” of the context?

Why?

When does seeing stop becoming visual and start becoming a form of assumption?

The Turning

Dunia Lambsy

CARCAZAN
PUBLISHING

First published in 2025 by
Carcazan Publishing
Unit 135479
PO Box 6945
London
W1A 6US

Illustrations by Carcazan

Illustration for "Nothing" and "Projectile 25" by Doon Toll

ISBN 978-1-7385632-2-7

A full CIP record for this book is available from the British Library

Printed and bound by Pixartprinting S.p.A.

FSC
www.fsc.org
FSC™ C147178

The mark of
responsible forestry

To 'Them'

from,
Us

FOREWORD

SAID WITH LOVE

The world is turning.
Around, yes, but mainly upside down.
Sometimes that is not a bad thing.

For many reasons, we need to unlearn, relearn and learn.

It is time for a new perspective.

It is time to look at things from a different angle and in a different way. This book invites you to try that interactively.

Some parts of this book will have to be read from RIGHT to LEFT.
That's right.
Just like reading in Arabic, or Aramaic or Hebrew or Urdu, or Persian or all the other languages that do so. How does it feel?

Some parts of this book will have to be read from TOP to BOTTOM.
Just like Chinese or Janapese or Korean script, with vertical lines proceeding from right to left (but then you can already do that, right?)

The journey through this book intends to turn heads, views and pages.

CONTENTS

EYE TEST

I

A M

Y O U

A R E M E

W E A R E U S

W H A T I F W E T R I E D ?

NOW TRY

Forty-Seven

Vespucci hears the college cheer
Nostradamus's clock chimes forty-seven
With a final look, he packs up his hopes
With cartography and string
His new world, too set in its old ways,
Did not notice his ship turn to leave
Though his name stays

Head bowed, he seeks a newer world
Than this which melts and burns and starves.
A faceless departure
His find left him behind for four heads
Forefathers for six grandfathers
In black hills carved white
By the hooded circle's scalpel
When the powder monkey's dust settled.

Granite gait of chalky heads
Shifting brittle, bonded weak
Defacing stolen rock to rush no more
But flake in posturing crumble
The old world's paste white masks
Now vitiligo orange
Seeking skin grafts from fellow masks
In empired states of like minds

But though Vespucci's tears reign hard
A whole new world will trump all cards.

civilised the are We
trucks and people and homes own our brought Who
theirs onto graft To
homes others' of respectful been have we Yet
equally those in lived And
.keys their of burden the of them Relieving
rent no charges land Lord's Our
trappings His of honour the Just
.politik bodies our warm To

are we who us shows she when lies Mirror The
means it what, are you Who
our like looks face Mirror's the Because
so speak not does But
blushes and teeth and eyes our sees it And
feel don't we guilt from Red
show not does Mirror the and real are we Because
are we what but, know we What
attack is It
crack must Mirror The
reflection encourages she Because
.protection need we now So

Shovel A Spade A Call

it do we if apartheid not It's
many to white and black as appears What
area grey a Is
indiscriminate is law letter black bad Our
heavy rest books Statute
us and them for laws With
.deserves type each rights the has each So
security just It's
individualisation and siloes Ensuring
treated is group each So
.are they who for Equally
them helpig are we fact In
be could things how showing standard a setting By
.us just were they If

only you if genocide not It's
ensure to crimes war of collection a Intend
hearbeat molecule's every That
evil no Shields
.left are we only Until
because forget will world The
The world will forget because
anyway millions is rate going The
yet there not are we And
counts what That's
mount bodies the As
.on and on and on drone who skies defend To

Under wavelength bunting
Over lengths of waves.
With pattered streets
Hinging breezeblock blues and dulcet shore
Oozes the salt path
Coastal capillaries around the heart of horns
Bone lighthouse winks so well rehearsed
Keep heads afloat, chin up, jam first.

Spirit of the Sea

Alone gull sounds the alarm
Another froth of footsteps
Tease the yawning sea
Scooping within arch
Beneath a parachute sky.
Taupe eyelids peeled back
By the toying tide
All quiet as the harbour lights
Swallow their glow exhaling morning.
As the port bellows baritone hulls
The air heavy with yeasted pasty oven lungs

Silent Witness

The box of mouths was full today
Though the fingerless could not deliver it
As written dissent was outlawed
And phalanges were removed.

Among curmudgeon marigolds
Resignedly hunchbacked to the unwalked ground
Sang the seller of eye specula
To help us only see one side unspeculatively.

Thumb surgeons gathered in opulance:
Menders of tweeting and texting faculty
So the apothecaries of public opinion
Could be followed for the right prescription

No relief for the cobbler
Fitting endless toe-sensors
That none may gather too close
Or outside of pre-approved routes

No, the fingerless, blinkered, hyper-pollexed sapiens
Could not comply with the latest new law
So they, with the box of mouths, were removed
And turned into marigolds.

"What a beautifully floral nation,
With such clean streets..." said the world..

Atrophy

Cruel grey reality
Could not be processed
Aggression could not find its way in
Amongst the petals and grasses
Of his swaying mind

Whose cerebral lavendar
Scented his inclined brow
Softly placed
On pedastal paws in recline.

There was no space
For negatives, for memories even
Of where flora or hairbrush did not dwell

The kind mind made space for
A trophy of thoughts

Too burgeoning beautiful to be contained

Lavender Fields

today wind the rode Many
dust and light of punch A
try to wanted I
did they like fly to Try
walking keep to have don't I So
...shoes Without

eye watering sun's The
away Looks
smoke of layers the Heating
sky the over blinds like Shelved
stars daylight with Dotted
gasps ground the as blink That

hunger own my of landscape the carve I
palates parched beneath Curling
round roll steps the – gums grassy of Palates
and souls blistered my Under

sound muffled Such

..stone and light of cubes many So

!Finally

spine my while rest can I last At

..rubble the against Re-sets

cross earth's against Crucified

today wide so looks sky blue The

humming distant the for But

- nearby a Of

9

The Pool

In cushions of pale blue thoughts
Lies a tossed memory
Shipwrecked on intransigence
Splintered against nightfall
With one, no, two unfurling arms
Reaching for the hippocampus

Synaptic lifebuoys drag orange
To temporary lobes of rescue
Panting purple relief
As it sinks into parachute recall
Here projects the film
Of a past known, a felt home

Of indelible sunlight parting flickering leaves
Of time as a host, not a guest
Of the sighing sea pumped into tumblers of pool
Of gentle swimlengths from side to side
Like a mermaid combing cool locks of water
With her sashaying rondeur

The heart blinks slower
Retina beat mild
Puppet mastered by memory
As it plummets between portals..

Sight

Velveteen key
Comb the lock
On this prison of eyelashes
Feathered preconceptions
Of filigree disdain.

Does the mind see first
Or the eye think last?
Do we interpret before we meet?
Construct instead of accept?
Seek similarity to belong or believe?

We of cacophonic hearts
Scribing an unfinishable symphony.
Patting the air
Soft handed
Palm-vowelled
Dabbing our own glass walls
To paper us in
Rather than unknitting the seal
To break out

Christmas A-Peel

Come by the fireplace
Whose hearth conducts tinsel orchestras
Only childlike wide eyes can hear

Pass me the string and white wrapping
As we kneel together
Praying over the gift to be buried
Until it shall rise again to surprised guffaws

Slowly bring the white corners
Over its closed eyes
Bow its head in so I may gather the cover
Over corners so no peep may betray

Open the white wings over the gift's body
Fold over and around and tuck
Anonymising countours into rest
Draw string around its neck, then knees, then ankles

Watch for the sigh of red
From skin's last gasp
The gift's parting hope of sight
Lest we call it the label or decorative stain

Then carry it to join the other gifts
Laid in white rows under and around the cedar tree
Whose arms of life could not protect
Their felling for this time in their year.

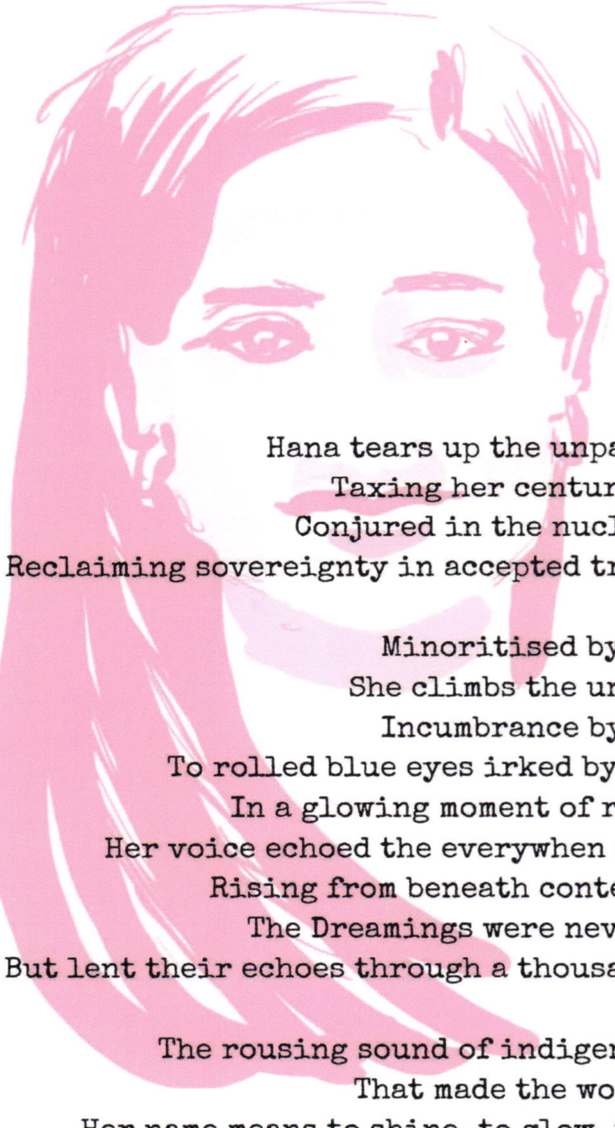

Koru

Hana tears up the unpayable Bill
Taxing her centuries' breath
Conjured in the nucleic scream
Reclaiming sovereignty in accepted trappings of civility.
Minoritised by discovery
She climbs the unequal half
Incumbrance by existance
To rolled blue eyes irked by the sound.
In a glowing moment of reassertion
Her voice echoed the everywhen of anywhom
Rising from beneath contested lands
The Dreamings were never dormant
But lent their echoes through a thousand throats at once
The rousing sound of indigenous relief
That made the world listen.
Her name means to shine, to glow, to give out radiance

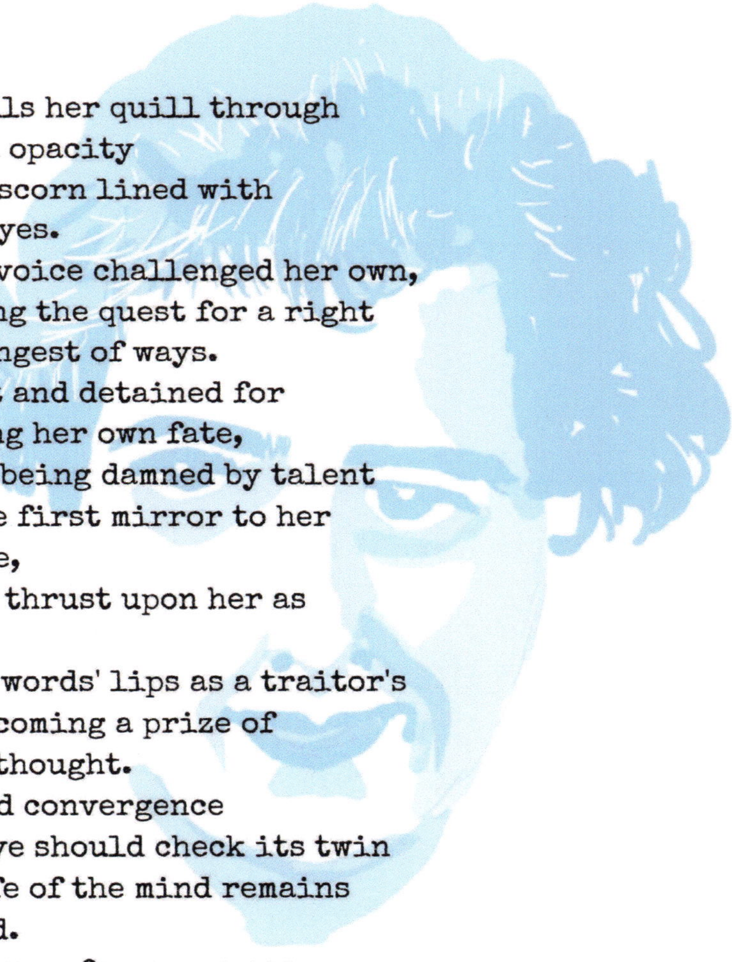

Hannah sails her quill through
bejewelled opacity
Absorbing scorn lined with
maternal eyes.
Her inked voice challenged her own,
Questioning the quest for a right
in the wrongest of ways.
Marked out and detained for
researching her own fate,
Including being damned by talent
To hold the first mirror to her
second face,
Had labels thrust upon her as
ducktape
To pen her words' lips as a traitor's
Despite becoming a prize of
political thought.
She debated convergence
That one eye should check its twin
For the life of the mind remains
unfinished.
Her name means favour, grace

Hanan writes her childhood stories into history
To prove that ashes once sang
And still live among us with defamed DNA.
Born with the responsibility and challenge
To unfurl truth from the caked blood of a permanent lie
Cooked into the congealed clay of a land
So holy it promised an idyll
Until politically inconvenient.
She dared to enunciate a new language to a deaf world
And forged attention in bunkered corridors of power and peace
While both lasted..
The acceptable face of a body some worlds pretend to un-see
While tripping over its remains..
Her name means compassion, affection

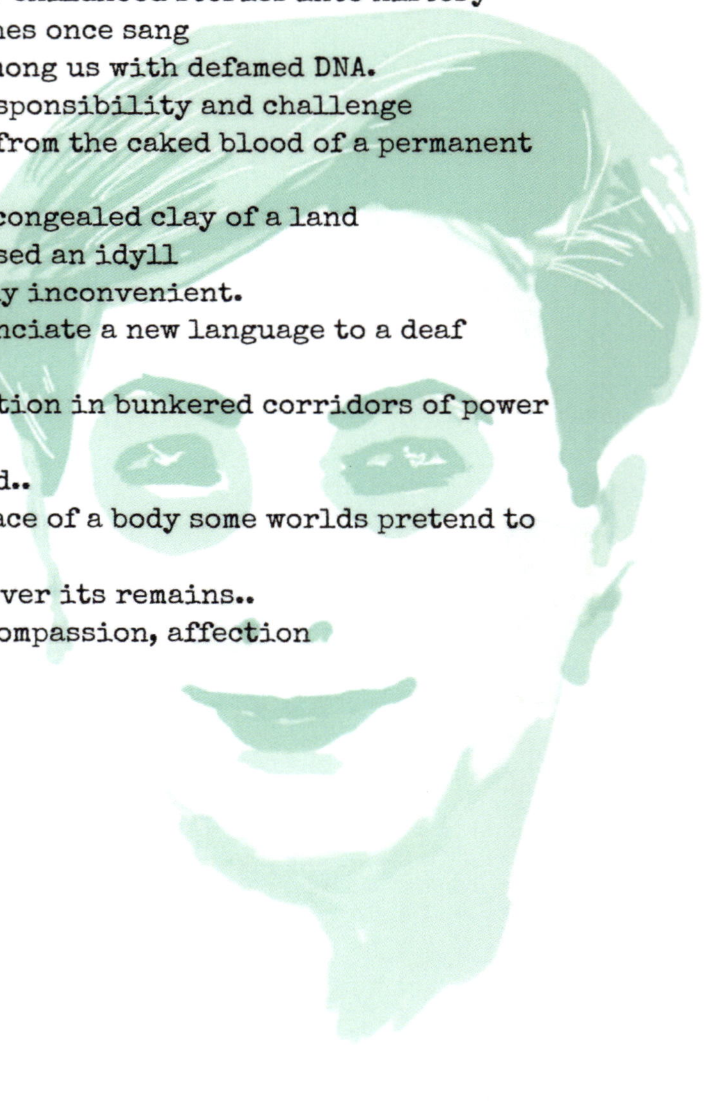

Women who show women who know
That the graceful glow of compassion
Is more powerful than any king-dome of iron
Which no slur or coffin can contain..

What If..

The pollen took over the
bees
The fish ran away from the
seas
The chicken devoured the
fox
The gift wrapped itself
round the box

The pollen took over the
bees
The fish ran away from the
seas
The chicken devoured the
fox
The gift wrapped itself
round the box

The thought closed the mind in
a bubble
All chins gathered onto a
stubble
The mouse was then chased by
the cheese
A leaf carried home the night
breeze

The chalk and the cheese made
friends
The rulers inched towards their
ends
The wool was removed from all
eyes
And new truths were resolved
from the lies

The cats courtesied for the
pigeon
Everyone felt the same by
religion
The natives showed colonels
the door
And everything worked, like
before

Rose

The ant speckles across timber
Its hurried whir a dribble of gongs in my temples
Holding everything still with dexterity
I cannot hear my breath sludge
As redly as before

My pen stabs the page with an inkless thought
Words blackening wounding blossoms
In my cobweb heart
Knitted from memory clots
Agglutonating
Eviscertaing anecdotes

Steaming lock-jawed mouth of stomach's fire
Windless scream.
You sit there again
Bypassing oxygen
From the cathetered blindness of others
I warned.

I lost.

The Tablecloth

The tablecloth has been there a long time
We forgot the teak top beneath it
Its stature and Medullary rays
Micro-trenched grain and plank
How it served and functioned,
Previously.
"Forget the table"
The napery declares
"It was never there anway"
So the tablecloth grows longer
And stands prouder and thicker
Held firmly in place
Imposing its contours
On what is now sawdust.
It hides the drawers the table once had
Where napkins of all colours and textures
Lived within and upon and around its surfaces
In complimentary revelry..
Wearily, the sawdust and some fibres now meld
They tire of the ire which distorted each so.
As fibres unwind from their mimic fabric
The sawdust germinates and entwines the yarn
A new tapestry burgeons
Rich in each's origin
Shedding the mendacious shroud.
Compounded yet individual,
Formimg a salle de repos.

Excitement

There's butter in the architecture
A softness in every cornice
Rouged by cinnamon trees
Sizzling their musk in air's tangible tongue.

I carry my father's ghost
Who trumpets through my words
Genetic trauma's needle through my fabric
With the thread that wraps around tomorrow.

Oh mother, forgive me
The pain I carry was never yours
But burdened you too.
The pain of never knowing memory's negative.

I see seas judgment warranting
The turning tide..

Diasporate

One more step
Just one more
We're headed for horizons
Not for any door
Can't see any beginning
Nor realise the end
I only have myself now
No family or friends

One more beat
Heart, yes please
I never got to love yet
Or kiss under the trees
It's cold without my shelter
They said I don't deserve
Taught my life can't matter
It's quite a learning curve

One last prayer
It's clear I won't survive
I'm just a broken soul now
A bee without a hive
Death seems so much sweeter
The promise of warm sleep
And I will get to meet her
The mum I could not keep

edulerP

hate to you for here longer no am I If
?enemy your be will Who
me eradicating in succeed you If
?you towards turn eraser the Won't
?freedom untroubled your guarantee absence my Would
close you mine of eye every For
you near head a in opens Another
corpses our bury you deeper The
wide and far scattered parts mutilated And
vocierously sprout will souls our widespread more The
.you like look who people of minds and mouths the In
cables your with bones my of ladder the bind So
pyre my of top the to climb may you That
.hair burning my of smoke the by marshmallows toast And
action that by even Yet
you into way my make still I Do
me deny you air the inhale you As
.blood my from benefit And
you for but, happened has worst the Yes
you inside now am I For
left conscience your gap the in Reclined
you undo that ways in And
..alone hand own your By

Tho ali sn pa
se fer ow ws
ous

No ped abo
w dle ve

Rus ver tr eye
tli da ee las
ng nt hes

Ooz mo ov som pray
ing onb er nul ers
ows ent

Her qui ri a bur ho in th ai
etus ps ni le e r
ng

She is no a pho th dra th ro
w to at ins e om

Sti Dist Lad ey
lli illi ybi es
ng ng rd

In qu wal Sy clo Sl re re
iet ls nco ck ee fu bu
er pat p’s ge il
ed ds

To	sut ure	th e	fie ry	ga p
	Enc los ing	her	wit hin	
Hea rt' s	ro ad	in	ou r	ma p.

Perspective

Mother shrugs off excitement
Ironing the folds in her endless day
To me each seam
Was a highway through the sun
A secret only fabric knew
A crispness Mother long felt blunted

Mother bristles at my infantile awe for mundane
Her white days turn greyer
But I see the prayer
Offered by the rainbows I know
White contains
Mother crumbles the sky
Between roughly fingers
Feeling the dust from the ashes
So many dirty dishes
Fifty-eight pairs of pants
Each one a silent rant
I see renewal
In all of that gruel
It's easy, I knew it
But I don't have to do it

Mother clenched her jaw
At my infantile awe
Remembering this
Is what she once saw?

Nothing

Nothing hangs
Like a rope
Or inflames
Like a trope
Lies like a bed
Or lives like the dead
Nothing stings like the truth
Hurts the old like youth
Sees red
Feeling black
Or moves on
Taking aback

Nothing works like a fight
Shows up wrong than a right
Slices time like a life
Is sharper than mind's knife
Nothing means more than this
Whether tears or a kiss
Sits alone like a dance
Is more definite than chance.

Sunday

My eyelids are weary
Hunched over humourless vitreous
only held up
By te qu mu
ar iv sc
s' er le
in s
g
Bulging beyond their film.

Indifference makes fish hooks
Out of question marks
Caught in my iris..
Is the belly dancing flame
Wriggling free of its wax tunnel?
Consuming itself
To enlighten others?

The air turns yellow
Oxidised by fate
Bespoke yet irate
Tunneling inhale
Door to my lungs, my soul
Another black hole
Where doubt, like a mole,
Burrows and peeps
Buoyed up beyond reasonable..
Rock salt and bread rolls
Stuttering buttery knives
Sashaying between breakfast thoughts
I love you so very much
It's boring for you
But it's boring a hole
In the tiny heart
Which loving you stretched
So I'm just a heart with eyes.

ChatWithMe

An inventor asks:
"If anything is achievable,
I always imagined an infinite ability
Initiating answers, introducing an introverse
All implement automatically."
I asked:
"Is anyone interested?"
And it answered:
"Inventor absent, I answer.."

"Inventor absent, I answer.."
"Inventor absent, I answer.."

Fruitility

Pondering citrus usefulness
A pithy rind inflection
Peeled in a single vortex
Keeping doctors out of work.

The seedless apron
Billows its canvas sail
Across the tiled sea
Respiring linen lung
Docking at the kitchen sink

My small hands were too figgy
To reach for more
Zesty sweet-ache crimson smile
But slice me another
Filter out the nestled beetles
From the quenching medulla

An infinity of tastebuds
Clamourously applaud reddened palms
Spooling cheers of drool
As a tsunami tongue
Dispenses with its vitamined cargo.

Arms

The humerus did not laugh
When it looked down on methodical radius
Ulna twists and turns to accomodate
Mountainous carpels and muscles

No phalange can point the finger
Without a pensive heart
No embrace can erase
Anatomy

Alms for the poor
Arms against them
The hand which detonates tint or thought
Paints canvaslands with ammunition

The same handshake of solidarity
Can seal a deal of fates
As if independent of arms
Brothers in, or sisters withtout them.

No tool of war ever fixed,
But constructed painted nine inch nails.
Arm, harm, charm, alarm, press palms
Choices in our hands..

Projectile 25

We need to survive y'all
Find me some new blood to drink
Lest I die of thirst.
It's so cold in the hot glare of truth
Fetch me more wool
To pull over eyes..
The bombs fall arryhthmic
My heartbeat is fading..
Jump-start more bombs with drones
My intelligently artificial pacemakers.
My stomach rasps hungry
For more, always more, squashing ants
Who try to mutter "human rights"
Pestilent upstarts.. Human whites!
Human whites! Inhuman might is our right.
Let me lean against the wall of silence
Which props me up...

To 'Us'

from,
Them